Boosting Your Self-Confidence

Compiled from Teenage Magazine

BOOKS

Group

Loveland, CO

Boosting Your Self-Confidence

Copyright © 1989 by Thom Schultz Publications, Inc.

First Printing

Credits
Edited by Lee Sparks
Illustrated by Jean Bruns
Designed by Judy Atwood Bienick
Cover photo by David Priest

Scripture quotations are from the Holy Bible, New International Version. Copyright © 1973, 1978, 1984 International Bible Society. Used by permission of Zondervan Bible Publishers.

Boosting your self-confidence : practical ways to feel better about the you God created : how to build your self-esteem, confidence, and productivity / compiled from Teenage magazine.
    p.   cm.
  ISBN 0-931529-90-5 : $5.95
  1. Teenagers—Religious life. 2. Self-respect—Religious aspects—Christianity. 3. Self-respect.   I. Teenage magazine (Loveland, Colo.)
BV4531.2.B66 1989
248.8'3—dc20   89-34149
                                   CIP

Printed in the United States of America

Contents

Introduction

Confidence: The Art of Trusting Yourself

. . . .

"If I could be God for just a few seconds, the one thing I would grant to people would be the ability to feel better about themselves."
—Taz W. Kinney

Nearly all of us as children were told the story, *The Little Engine That Could*. We remember Mom or Dad or a teacher reading to us about the little blue train engine who repeated, "I think I can, I think I can" when asked if she could pull a heavy train over a mountain. She does, of course, and then exclaims, "I thought I could, I thought I could!"

The purpose of *Boosting Your Self-Confidence* is to help you develop an "I think I can" spirit. As you know, it's sometimes hard to feel confident. We get pressure from school, work and home to do better—to be better. Yet our biggest foe in our quest for self-confidence is most often ourselves. We can suffer from low self-worth, which discourages us from doing our best, and *that* can lead to a sense of hopelessness. But this is not God's will for you. God wants you to enjoy the you that he made. He wants you to live in confidence. "Be confident of this, that he who began a good work in you will carry it on to completion until the day of Christ Jesus" (Philippians 1:6).

These chapters originally appeared in Teenage Magazine (formerly Group Members Only). They have helped many young people grow in God's gift of confidence. May God give you confidence in who you are and the life you live.

Section One
Building Confidence: The You God Made

Chapter 1
Feeling Good About Yourself

Lisa hates her looks. On a scale of one to 10, she thinks she's a minus five. She's too tall, her hair's frizzy and her clothes are out of style. Lisa wanted a new wardrobe for school this year, but she didn't start saving money soon enough. So she's stuck with clothes that make her feel like a reject from a movie made in the 1950s.

All that might not be so bad if she had an outgoing personality. But Lisa's painfully shy; she's never sure what to say around other people. When she does work up the courage to say something, it usually comes out wrong. And it always happens around the "perfect people" at school—like Amy Anderson. Amy is petite, beautiful and always wears stylish and expensive clothes. When Amy's around, Lisa feels like an alien from Mars.

We *all* suffer from poor self-esteem sometime in our lives. And many of us, like Lisa, find it distorting our thoughts and actions. The fact that God created us and is delighted with us as we are (Ephesians 1:11) doesn't stop us from looking at ourselves and deciding nothing's right. It isn't long before we convince ourselves we need a complete make over.

If that's how you sometimes feel, read on. You'll see how easy it is to let your self-esteem slip, and how several simple steps will get you feeling good about yourself again.

► Self-Esteem Torpedoes

We use self-esteem torpedoes to shoot ourselves down until there's nothing left but dissatisfaction. And three of our most common torpedoes are comparison, criticism and unrealistic goals.

● **Comparison.** One of Lisa's biggest problems is that she compares herself to others—and always comes up short. When you see someone who's good-looking, talented or wealthy, it's only normal to compare yourself to that person. But carrying the comparison too far is unwise, because you get down on yourself for not being as good, or as fortunate, as someone else. The feeling that you don't measure up can eat away at you and poison your feelings of self-worth.

● **Criticism.** Criticizing yourself is a common response to unfavorable comparison. But *constant* criticism makes it almost impossible to believe in or even like yourself. When all you hear—from yourself or others—are negative comments, you eventually believe them.

Criticism can become a weapon against others,

too, when you try to build yourself up by knock-
ing others down. A comment like "Yeah, he's
good-looking, but he's got the brains of an aard-
vark" may be funny the first time, but constantly
cutting others down can backfire. No one likes to
be around a person who's always critical or sarcastic, so you soon may find yourself being left
out and feeling bad.

● **Unrealistic goals.** Lisa sabotaged her new
wardrobe by not giving herself enough time to
save the money she needed. Did you ever fail to
give yourself enough time to accomplish a goal?
When you realized you weren't going to make it,
how did you feel? Rotten, probably. When you
set goals, base them on a realistic evaluation of
your circumstances, time and abilities. Wanting to
be the top varsity basketball player can be a
good goal, if you have the gifts and skills to succeed on the court. Setting yourself up for failure
is a sure way to undermine healthy self-esteem.

► Good Feelings

Realizing you're special to God, just as you are,
is the first step toward a healthier self-image.
Then work to develop a positive attitude, to
build others up and to laugh at yourself. Taking
the "Self-Awareness Inventory" in this chapter
will also give you a lift.

● **Cultivate a positive attitude.** Look
around you. God's given you a whole world to
enjoy. Although things may not be perfect, you
can find something good in each day—a hug
from a friend, beautiful weather, the assurance of

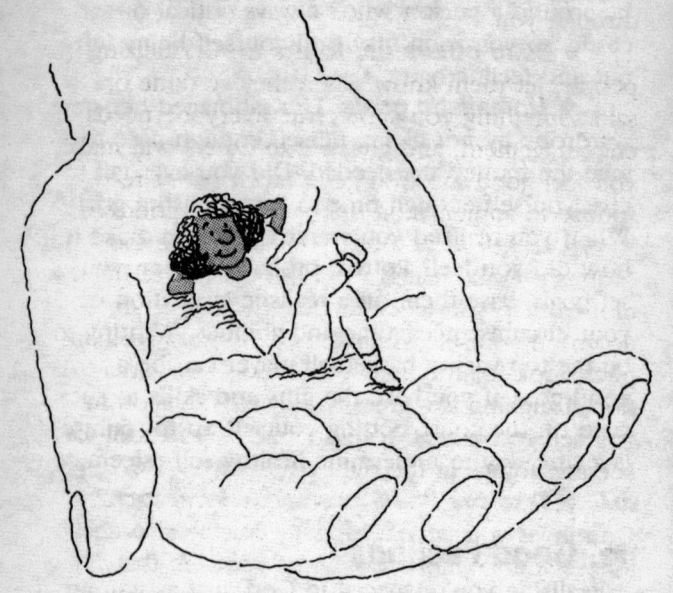

God's kid

God's presence. Also, realize that you are who you are because of God, and he knows what he's doing. Don't waste time looking for your short-comings. Face each day with the assurance that God's going to do something special for and through you.

● *Build others up.* Rather than criticizing people, let them know when they've done or said something you appreciate. Everyone needs encouragement, and giving it to others will make you feel good too. You get a much better re-sponse to appreciation than you do to criticism.

● *Laugh at yourself.* Don't take life too seriously. God created you with a sense of hu-mor to help you enjoy life. Instead of getting down on yourself when something negative hap-pens, look for the humorous side of the situa-tion. Laughing is a great way to ease tension in yourself and others. It's also an excellent tool for keeping things in the right perspective.

● *Take the "Self-Awareness Inventory."* God loves you unconditionally, but he also chal-lenges you to improve areas of your life that aren't all he wants them to be. He invites you to look at yourself honestly—see your real strengths and weaknesses. Then let him show you what needs changing.

Use the "Self-Awareness Inventory" in this chapter to take an honest look at yourself. You may be surprised at how many good things you'll find out about yourself. Then read through the rest of this book for more ways to grow self-esteem and confidence. You'll be amazed how God will help you become an even more terrific person.

Remember, your worth isn't determined by your clothes, your looks or even your personality. Your worth lies in the fact that God created you as someone special and he loves you—strengths, weaknesses and all.

Karen Ball

Self-Awareness Inventory

Think about the physical, spiritual, emotional, social and intellectual aspects of your life; then fill in the chart below by listing both your good and not-so-good points.

When you're done, look at your list of not-so-good points and determine the things you're able to change. For example, you can change your tendency to interrupt others, but you can't do a lot about the size of your feet.

The Two Sides of Me

	Good Points	Not-So-Good Points
Physical:		
Spiritual:		
Emotional:		
Social:		
Intellectual:		

continued

Next, fill in the "Do It!" box. Write those things you're willing to work on changing. This isn't a "wish" list; it's a "get it done" list. Pray about each item on your list; then set up a specific, realistic plan for change.

Do It!
I'm willing to work hard to change these things about myself.

I'll change this . . .

to this . . .

by doing this . . .

by this date . . .

Tell your goals to a friend and ask that person to help you stick to your plan. It helps to know you're accountable to someone who cares.

Now, put your list of goals somewhere you'll look often; for example, on your mirror. And remember, let God guide your efforts. He wants you to succeed as much as you do, and he won't let you down.

Chapter 2
No Good or Too Good?

Jennifer's friends have stopped giving her many compliments. It's not that Jennifer doesn't appreciate their compliments. The problem is she likes them too much—and adds to them. If a friend congratulates her on getting an A on a math test, Jennifer says something like, "It's about time someone noticed how good I am in math. I work harder than just about anyone in the class." Then she walks away without even saying goodbye.

In contrast, David quietly goes about his business at school. He's one of those people who rarely says anything. They look at the floor if someone looks at them and seem unexcited about anything. Like Jennifer, David earned an A on the math test. But if another student were to congratulate him, David would say, "I just got lucky I guess. I'm really not that smart. You're probably better in math than I am."

God wants you to believe in yourself and feel good about your abilities. Believing you're a worthy person doesn't mean you're a snob, and being humble isn't the same as feeling worthless. Jennifer and David both suffer from a lack of confidence. Jennifer reveals her insecurities by broadcasting how great she is, appearing "stuck up." David shows his insecurities by denying or discounting his abilities.

► Rate Your Self-Confidence

It's great having self-confidence. But do you ever wonder if you're acting conceited? Or do you sometimes put yourself down to feel humble?

Try this evaluation to see if your self-confidence is over-inflated or tainted by false humility. For each situation, circle the answer that most closely represents your response.

1. When someone asks me what my talents are, I:

    (a) can't think of any. _____

    (b) thank God because he gave them to me. _____

    (c) feel I have more gifts than others. _____

2. When someone compliments me, I:

    (a) feel embarrassed and make excuses. _____

    (b) point out how I'm gifted in this area. _____

    (c) say "thank you." _____

3. When I make a mistake, I:
   (a) get up and start again, knowing I'm human. _____
   (b) feel like a complete failure. _____
   (c) blame someone else. _____

4. When I'm with my friends, I:
   (a) try to be who they want me to be. _____
   (b) feel comfortable being myself and enjoy their company. _____
   (c) believe I should help them get their act together. _____

5. When I look at my weaknesses, I:
   (a) accept them as part of who I am. _____
   (b) feel they keep me humble. _____
   (c) think I'm no worse than the next guy. _____

6. When people ask me to do something I don't agree with, I:
   (a) give in so I'm not laughed at. _____
   (b) say "I'm sorry; that wouldn't be right for me." _____
   (c) tell them they're stupid. _____

7. When a friend does something well, I:
   (a) feel jealous of his or her talent. _____
   (b) think I could have done just as well. _____
   (c) enjoy complimenting him or her. _____

8. When I wear the latest fashion, I:
  (a) feel confident about looking my best.
  _____

  (b) feel more accepted by others. _____
  (c) feel that I set the fashion pace among my
      friends. _____

Self-Confidence Scoring

For each question, give yourself the following
number of points. Total your points when you're
through.

1. (a) 1 (b) 2 (c) 3
2. (a) 1 (b) 3 (c) 2
3. (a) 2 (b) 1 (c) 3
4. (a) 1 (b) 2 (c) 3
5. (a) 2 (b) 1 (c) 3
6. (a) 1 (b) 2 (c) 3
7. (a) 1 (b) 3 (c) 2
8. (a) 2 (b) 1 (c) 3

Add Up Your Self-Confidence Score

20-24 points: Oh oh! Your self-confidence is
over-inflated.
13-19 points: Great! You have a well-balanced attitude.
8-12 points: Ouch! You need a self-confidence
boost.

What did you learn about yourself in the quiz?
Do you think you're too good? no good? The Bible has a lot to offer for building a healthy view
of ourselves. Paul said, "Do not think of yourself
more highly than you ought, but rather think of
yourself with sober judgment, in accordance

with the measure of faith God has given you" (Romans 12:3). Here are some guidelines for developing a more balanced view of yourself:

● *Recognize your uniqueness.* You're an original combination of strengths and weaknesses, a handmade original stamped "God's idea." So celebrate your uniqueness.

● *Thank God for your abilities.* Your talents and abilities come from God, and thanking him doesn't make you stuck-up or inferior. Your gratitude gives God the credit. List your strengths and dedicate them to God.

● *Learn from your mistakes.* We all make mistakes, so don't focus on them. Instead ask yourself why you blew it. Then look for help to correct and understand your mistakes. Next time, you'll be prepared.

● *Accept your weaknesses.* Write down your weaknesses and pray about them. Ask God to use your weaknesses to show his strength. Then change what you can and accept what you can't.

● *Don't compare yourself with others.* Competition weakens your self-confidence. You'll always find others who are better at something, so don't compare yourself to them. Look to God for your standard. He approves of you the way you are.

● *Take a stand.* Part of self-confidence is standing up for what you believe. Develop values and defend them. That means at times you'll have to say no to situations you don't agree with, such as using drugs or disobeying your parents. Your friends will respect you, and you'll respect yourself.

● *Build up your friends.* Look for the best in others. Tell friends you appreciate them. Give sincere compliments, send cards or give hugs.

● *Focus on the inside, but look your best.* Take time to look good, but also spend time with God daily. Remember clothes, makeup and money don't make you; God does. Pray that God will mold you to be more like him each day.

Berry Richardson

Chapter 3
Hi, I'm Ugly

I have a friend who's probably one of the ugliest kids in high school. Cal's chin protrudes from his face like a doorknob. And his Adam's apple looks like it's competing with his chin for attention. From time to time, Cal allows a few stray whiskers to grow a little too long on his Adam's apple—making it look like a porcupine meatball. Cal's eyes are deep-set. If the light strikes him just right, his eyes disappear into dark shadows, like they aren't there at all—like a skull.

A lot of kids laugh at Cal. Most of them don't mean to be cruel. It's just that Cal looks like a cartoon character. And most cartoon characters look funny.

One person laughs at Cal louder than anyone else, and that's Cal himself. His last name is Robinson, but Cal calls himself "Robin-chin" in honor of the bulbous thing on the bottom of his face. He didn't coin that name himself; some other jokester did. But Cal thought it was a lot funnier than the common name of Robinson.

► Cal's Secret

Cal has discovered a real secret. He's not only learned to accept himself, with all of his imperfections—he's learned to laugh at himself. And he's one of the happiest guys I know.

During the teenage years, we gaze in the mirror a lot. The poor mirror has to listen to stuff like "I have the biggest ears in the whole school," "This nose is pathetic," "Oh, no, another zit—that makes 394, not counting the ones on my back" and "You're ugly, you know that?"

How many times have you asked the mirror what it would cost for a face transplant? If only you could look like a movie star.

But what fun would it be if everyone looked like a movie star?

► Your Uniqueness

Your body is like your personality—it's unique, one of a kind, a gift from God. Think of it. Celebrate!

If it's your floppy ears that set you apart from everyone else, celebrate! If it's your big nose, celebrate!

Paul, in his letter to the Corinthians, said: "Do you not know that your body is the temple of the Holy Spirit, who is in you, whom you have received from God? You are not your own; you were bought at a price. Therefore honor God with your body" (1 Corinthians 6:19-20).

Your body is a temple. It belongs to God. And God doesn't go around creating a bunch of eyesores for temples. He never meant for the inhabi-

tants of these temples to spend their time worrying about how ugly they think the architecture is.

Every temple is different. Every temple is beautiful.

If you think you have an appearance that the
rest of the world would label "ugly," remember . . . your body is a special gift from God.
And that gift helps you become a better person
on the inside. Jesus said, "Whoever exalts himself
will be humbled, and whoever humbles himself
will be exalted" (Matthew 23:12). Your overhang-
ing forehead or fat lips may be just what helps to
keep you humble in a world that often worships
beauty.

This isn't to say that you shouldn't exercise,
wash your hair, brush your teeth or wear clean
clothes. That part of the "temple appearance" is
up to you. But the features of your appearance
that are beyond your control are a part of you.
They make you unique.

▶ Self-Acceptance

The first step for all of us "ugly" people is ac-
cepting our uniqueness. Real self-acceptance is
kind of an inside job. It doesn't come by finding
someone who's "uglier" and teasing him or her
about it.

The next step is humor—not the kind of humor that belittles others for their looks, but Cal's
kind of humor.

Learning to laugh at yourself not only helps
you, it helps the people around you. Once other
people know you're not sensitive about your

So what if I'm not Joe Handsome?

looks, they'll feel a lot more comfortable around you. And that usually opens the door for them to look beyond your physical characteristics and into the real you. You'll discover that your uniqueness isn't something to be ashamed of, but something to celebrate.

Thom Schultz

Getting More Fun Out of Life

Humor is a gift from God. He gave it to us to help us enjoy the good times, and ease us through the bad times. But we have to learn to use our humor to make the most out of every situation we encounter.

Do you really use humor to get the most out of each moment? Find out. For each statement below, rate yourself by placing an "X" in the box in the column that best describes your answer.

Statements	None of the time	Some of the time	Most of the time
I enjoy silly, zany thoughts.	☐	☐	☐
I show an attitude of playfulness.	☐	☐	☐
I use my sense of humor to keep life in perspective.	☐	☐	☐
I laugh *with* others, not *at* others.	☐	☐	☐
I laugh at what people do—not who they are.	☐	☐	☐
I take time to enjoy things that help me laugh (comedies, jokes, fun friends).	☐	☐	☐
I laugh at myself instead of taking myself too seriously.	☐	☐	☐
I accept myself—shortcomings and all.	☐	☐	☐
I create a spirit of happiness when I'm around others.	☐	☐	☐
I believe I can "Rejoice in the Lord always" (Philippians 4:4) even though situations may trouble me.	☐	☐	☐
I believe God wants me to accept myself and enjoy life (John 10:10).	☐	☐	☐

continued

Scoring: If most of your "X's" landed under "Most of the time," you probably enjoy a positive sense of humor and a healthy life perspective.

If "Some of the time" holds most of your "X's," you probably find fun in life, but could raise your sense of humor by developing the areas you marked low.

If most of your "X's" show up under "None of the time," you probably need a shot of humor in your attitude. Surround yourself with positive people who have a good sense of humor. Dig into the scripture to understand the full life that God offers you. Make a list of situations that keep you from enjoying life; then think of ways to change them or your attitude toward them.

Situations:

Ways to change:

Chapter 4
Mirror, Mirror, on the Wall

Stretch. Pull. Pump iron until you can't pinch an inch. Stop when you drop.

Starve. Binge. Pig out and polish off a bag of chips. Curse the midnight munchies.

Sound familiar? If so, you're not alone. Shaping the perfect figure is frustrating. And it's hard work.

But are looks important? Yes, say many teenagers. Search Institute surveyed several thousand teenagers. And it found two worries top their list: their looks, and how well others like them. Other studies show that looks rank high on teenagers' list of worries.

It's easy to see why. When you click on the television, you watch the stars flaunt their lean figures. They never seem to bat an eyelash to keep the fat off and the muscles on.

Advertisements, magazines, newspapers and television keep telling you to look like these perfect heroes. Then when you look in your mirror every morning, you gasp. You never realized how bad you looked.

► Managing Your Mirror

By the time you turn 17, you'll have spent almost 18 months looking in the mirror. But do you ever think about who's telling you what to see in the mirror? Is it the media, holding a mirror that exaggerates your fat and zits? Or is it God, who shows you someone who reflects God's image?

Jill always looked in the media's mirror. She was a model, a Miss Teen contestant, an A student and a cheerleader. Her high school classmates insisted she was beautiful. But Jill never saw what they did. Instead, the high school junior saw only fat.

So she took diet pills, Ex-Lax—anything to help her lose weight. After two years, her weight dropped to 81 pounds. But Jill still didn't think she was beautiful.

Jill finally gave up. After taking painkillers, she doused herself with gasoline. Then she lit a match.

Jill isn't alone in her desperate attempt to get rid of the ugly fat the media's mirror always points out. Experts say eating disorders and dieting are two of the top six health problems teenagers face. As many as 15 percent of teenage girls suffer from bulimia or anorexia. And one out of eight 10th-graders tries to lose weight by vomiting, taking laxatives or using drugs.

► Beautifying Your Body

Even if you don't have a serious health problem like an eating disorder, you probably diet to improve your looks. The average person goes on a diet 10 times a year. And, in the process, supports a $15 billion diet industry.

"Dieting has become a new religion," says Edward J. Dumke, a California Episcopal priest. In his book, *The Serpent Beguiled Me & I Ate*, Dumke says diets lack two essential ingredients: hope and faith. "Each new diet becomes a new cult with a new promise of salvation," he says. And when a diet doesn't deliver the happiness it promises, you feel even worse than before you started.

Most diets simply don't work. Of people who diet, 95 percent gain back the weight they lose. Why? Because they return to their old eating habits.

In fact, most people gain back more weight after a diet. They reward themselves for losing weight by eating more! Dieting isn't the only way to change your looks. You may try many different ways. Some teenagers pay surgeons to suck out their extra fat with liposuction. This method, which costs $3,000 to $7,000, is the most popular plastic surgery for teenagers.

But most teenagers can't afford this surgery. So many of them hang out at the health club. Teenagers lift and row for hours, hoping to make their bodies slim and trim. They want to feel good about what they see in the mirror.

But bodies change slowly. And some bodies just aren't made to look like body builders'. But the media's mirror keeps insisting you look perfect. So you may choose another method to beef up your body.

That's what Bill did. Within a year, his weight increased by 100 pounds—in all the right places. Before that, Bill only made C's in school. He was too small to get on the football team. And few seemed to notice him at school.

But steroids made the difference. Not only did he make varsity football, but Bill's stronger body gave him self-confidence. For the first time, he could muster up the courage to ask a girl for a date. When she said yes, Bill was sure steroids had solved his problems.

But Bill soon discovered the girls were more interested in his biceps than him. So he exercised more and more. He took higher doses of steroids, hoping to get their attention.

Then Bill had his annual medical exam. He learned his blood pressure was dangerously high. If Bill didn't stop taking steroids, the doctor said, Bill could die of cancer or heart failure.

Bill's attempt to look better in the media's mirror failed to bring the love he wanted. And it threatened his life.

► Liking Your Looks

If dieting and body building don't change how you see yourself in the mirror, what can you do? You can change mirrors. One reason you don't like what you see in the media's mirror is because that mirror's distorted. It doesn't reflect who you really are. A much better mirror is

God's mirror. It reflects a person God formed in his image. So it shows you as you really are.

Luke 12:22-28 challenges you to have faith. And that faith includes not worrying about your body, clothes or food. Instead, it means letting go of those obsessions. It means learning to trust the God who loves you and meets your needs. And as you learn to trust God, you'll begin to see the same beauty in yourself that God gave to the lilies of the field.

So look at yourself in God's mirror. And smile. See that child of God who's loved and accepted despite heavy hips or sagging biceps. You're a beautiful person. And God loves you just the way you are.

Jolene L. Roehlkepartain

Seeing Yourself in the Mirror

Now that you've read the chapter, think about what *you* see in the mirror. Do you see fat? Or do you see muscles? Do you like your reflection?

Take this quiz and find out how you view your body.

Looking at Your Looks

Read each statement. Then circle the number that best represents how much you agree with the statement.

Circle "1" if you strongly agree, "2" if you agree, "3" if you neither agree nor disagree, "4" if you disagree, and "5" if you strongly disagree.

Be honest. Circle how you *feel*, not how you *think* you should feel.

Statements	Strongly agree				Strongly disagree
I wish I were better-looking.	1	2	3	4	5
If I built up my body, the opposite sex would find me more attractive.	1	2	3	4	5
I'd die without a summer tan.	1	2	3	4	5
I wish I could start an exercise routine.	1	2	3	4	5
I need to eat more nutritious foods.	1	2	3	4	5
I wear nice clothes to feel good about myself.	1	2	3	4	5
Whenever I pass a mirror, I always notice how I look.	1	2	3	4	5
I worry about getting fat.	1	2	3	4	5

continued

I feel pressured to look my best all the time.	1	2	3	4	5
I'm embarrassed about how I look in a swimsuit.	1	2	3	4	5
I need to lose (or gain) more weight.	1	2	3	4	5
I feel it's important to look attractive.	1	2	3	4	5
Before going out, I spend a lot of time getting ready.	1	2	3	4	5
I'm always changing fashions and hair styles to improve my looks.	1	2	3	4	5

When you finish, add up the numbers you circled. If you scored 36 or below, you're uptight about your body. You spend a lot of time trying to look better. Think of ways to spend less time in front of the mirror and more time feeling good about yourself.

If you scored 37 to 47, congratulations. You have a balanced view of your body. You think your body's important. But you don't spend all your time taking care of it.

If you scored 48 or above, you're avoiding your body. You may feel embarrassed about your looks. Or you may think looks aren't important. Spend a little more time taking care of your body so you can feel better about yourself.

Chapter 5
I'm Sick of Me!

A black gloom looms over you. You hate your looks. You feel like you don't have any friends. But that's not surprising. You can't stand yourself. So why would anyone else?

When you're unhappy with yourself, it colors everything you say and do. It affects your relationships with your family, with your friends—and with God.

It's funny, but disliking yourself acts like a virus. It creeps up on you subtly and then suddenly knocks you flat. And you can't cure it until you've identified the cause and taken proper medication. It's a virus that attacks your attitudes and causes you to feel inadequate, angry or depressed.

► Inadequacy Virus

You know, for a while I really thought I could make the cheerleading squad, Julee thought. I practiced and practiced. And my friends said I was pretty good at tryouts. So why didn't my name show up on the roster?

I could have died. All those other girls—the chosen ones—stood around giggling and screaming. And I just stood there reading the list over and over knowing they must have made a mistake.

And then, couldn't you have prevented this somehow, God? Sheryl Winston, captain of the squad, looked at me and said in that superior tone of hers: "Gee, Julee. Maybe next year. Don't let it bother you."

I wanted to crawl away and cry. I tried so hard. But I should have known better. I should have known I wouldn't be good enough.

Rejection of any kind is tough. No one likes to feel left out or unwanted. But when you take a rejection so seriously that you start feeling totally inadequate, you've welcomed the virus that will make you sick. The disease? Disliking yourself.

Stop this virus of feeling inadequate by looking at Psalm 139:13: "You [God] created my inmost being; you knit me together in my mother's womb." No doubt about it: You're a unique individual, a special creation. When God made you, he knew everything about you. Everything.

So don't worry about not measuring up. God put you together, inside and out. Look at what God has to say about you:

- You're God's child (John 1:12);
- You're precious (Isaiah 43:4);
- You're completely forgiven (Colossians 1:14);
- You're so important that God sacrificed his Son (John 3:16); and

● You have a wonderful life ahead (John 10:10).

Inadequate? Hardly. You're a masterpiece. God's masterpiece.

▶ Anger Virus

I know I shouldn't have yelled at Len. I mean, he's my best friend, Ivan thought. But when he said I was being obnoxious, I just lost it. Okay, so I've been a real grouch lately. And so I said some mean things about a few people. I wish I could take back what I said. But that doesn't give Len the right to call me obnoxious. Why can't he mind his own business and leave me alone?

Anger is probably the most common—and fastest acting—attitude virus of all. When you're dissatisfied with yourself, when you don't like yourself, it's next to impossible to like anyone else. And all it takes is someone saying or doing something a little bit wrong and you blow.

When this virus hits, follow the cure prescribed in Psalm 141:3: "Set a guard over my mouth, O Lord; keep watch over the door of my lips." Venting your frustration on someone else will only make matters worse and often make you dislike yourself even more. Instead, relieve your tension by playing tennis, racquetball, baseball or checkers. Go for a walk, run, swim or ride. Write how you feel.

Even better, find a good friend and tell him or her what's going on. You may discover that talking things out with someone who cares will relieve your inner tension and get you back on the right track.

► Depression Virus

God, I can't stand it anymore, Marta prayed. I can't stand me anymore. No matter how hard I try, I'm never good enough. I just don't measure up. It seems like I mess up everything I try.

I sprained my ankle and had to quit the gymnastics team. My best friend and I had a fight. My boyfriend is moving to another town. And my face is exploding with zits. (I know, I know, the five chocolate bars I ate after I yelled at my friend probably caused it, but it still doesn't seem fair.)

I mean, how am I supposed to do all the great things you want me to do, such as talk to people about you and your love, when all I can think about is how much I hate myself?

Have you ever felt like giving up because nothing was working out? This common reaction to the hassles in life often results in depression. You feel overwhelmed—even hopeless. You know deep inside that everything isn't awful, but you see so much bad that you've lost sight of the good. And you're sick of it all.

You'll find the cure for this attitude virus in Romans 8:28: "We know that in all things God works for the good of those who love him, who have been called according to his purpose." Think about it. In God's eyes you're somebody important. So important that God is watching what's happening to you—and he's got it under

God likes me the way he made me.

control.

You may not understand it right now; you may not even like it a whole lot; but hang in there. Someday God will turn the light on and you'll see and understand things a whole lot better.

So although you can't ever totally escape disliking yourself now and then, stop those attitude viruses cold. And when you do that, you'll discover a feeling of release and confidence—confidence that you can trust God.

Trust that God loves you. Trust that the stories written in the Bible aren't just a bunch of words. See that they're all promises you can put to work now, today, to cure yourself when you need it most.

Karen Ball

Evaluating Your Symptoms

When you think of yourself, do you feel good or bad? For each of the following statements, checkmark "True" or "False" to find out which ones could lead you to disliking yourself.

Statements	True	False
1. I think people like me only because I have a lot of friends, not because of who I am.	☐	☐
2. I worry a lot about doing stupid things around my friends because they'll think I'm dumb.	☐	☐
3. I'm afraid to talk with people because I always seem to say the wrong thing.	☐	☐
4. If I'm in a room full of people I don't know well, I usually stand off by myself because I'm not sure how to break the ice. Then afterward I get mad at myself for feeling this way.	☐	☐
5. I like the way I look.	☐	☐
6. When I try to do something and mess up, I realize that's just the way things go sometimes.	☐	☐

continued

7. I get mad when someone criticizes something I say or do. ☐ ☐

8. I hate hanging around popular people because I don't fit in. ☐ ☐

9. I'm comfortable in new or different situations. I like to get to know new people. ☐ ☐

10. When I'm in a group of strangers, I'm often one of the first people to start a conversation. ☐ ☐

Your Results

Give yourself 2 points for checking "True" or 1 point for marking "False" in numbers 1, 2, 3, 4, 7 and 8. For numbers 5, 6, 9 and 10, give yourself 2 points for each "False" and 1 point for each "True."

Add up your score. If you got 11 points or more, your symptoms suggest you may be suffering from a "disliking yourself" virus. You may compare yourself with others or worry too much about how others think of you.

Take a good look at yourself and see what you like about yourself. Then take the "Three-Step Cure" to help you realize you're someone worthwhile.

Three-Step Cure

Rx: Take these three steps to stop disliking yourself before the self-esteem virus starts.

1. Know yourself. When you start hating yourself, make a list of things you like about yourself. Consider your skills, talents, personality traits, spiritual state and even physical attributes.

Then go to your parents and ask them to tell you what they like about you. Let them know you're compiling a list to help you avoid disliking yourself. Then ask a couple of friends to do the same.

Finally, see what God says about you. Take a look at Jeremiah 29:11; 2 Corinthians 2:15; 5:20; Philippians 4:19; and James 1:5. Write the good things God says and thinks about you.

2. Accept yourself. Anytime you start getting down on yourself, go back to your list of good things. Read each item carefully, asking God to help you accept these attributes as true and valid. Accept that you're someone special in God's eyes. You're worth a lot to God, your family and your friends.

3. Let go. Ask God to take over your feelings and help you avoid getting bogged down in hating yourself. Ask God to show you what traits you may need to change and to help you do what you can to change them. Then once you turn something over to God, trust that he'll take care of things.

Remember, God made you as you are. And it's his desire that everything that happens to you will eventually work together for your good. Believe it! You can depend on God.

Chapter 6
A New Way of Thinking

Waking Up . . .

Rain . . . Monday . . . chem test first period. I hate rain. I hate Mondays. I hate chemistry. Why bother getting up? Same old weather. Same old Raisin Bran and milk. Same classes. Forever, peanut butter and jelly for lunch. Always Burger King from 4 o'clock to 7 o'clock. Standing on my feet, smiling at people I've never seen before and probably will never see again. Forget it all. I just want to sleep my way into oblivion . . .

God's Perspective:
"See, I am doing a new thing . . . " (Isaiah 43:19). *"This is the day the Lord has made; let us rejoice and be glad in it"* (Psalm 118:24).

Choosing Clothes . . .

Nothing to wear again. Never anything to wear. Can't afford much even though Mom and Dad both work. This is the third fall for this blue sweater. And Jenny James wears a new outfit almost every day. I'd have the dates *she* has if I had her wardrobe. Well, here goes the blue sweater again.

God's Perspective:
"Man looks at the outward appearance, but the Lord looks at the heart" (1 Samuel 16:7). *"See how the lilies of the field grow . . . if that is how God clothes the grass of the field . . . will he not much more clothe you . . . ?"* (Matthew 6:28-30).

Listening to Parents . . .

Cut the chatter. It's too early in the morning to be bombarded with details. So the yard needs mowing this evening and my scholarship application is due in the office by 9 a.m. I remember. Just get off my back and let me stare into my Raisin Bran in peace and quiet.

God's Perspective:
"Listen . . . to your father's instruction, and do not forsake your mother's teaching" (Proverbs 1:8).

Feeling Inferior . . .

There they are again. Right next to my locker. The "in" group. Smooth lines. "In" clothes. Tons of friends. Now I have to walk right by them. What do I say? I'm not witty or clever. Can't think of a great line if I try. "Nice weather isn't it?"—they'd laugh me right out of town. Why do I have to be so bland? A lump of nothing . . .

God's Perspective:
"You are precious and honored in my sight . . . I love you . . . " (Isaiah 43:4). *"He who began a good work in you will carry it on to completion until the day of Christ Jesus"* (Philippians 1:6).

Worrying About Failure . . .

Scholarships. Who do I think I am, applying for this scholarship? Only 100 other people apply for the same thing. Wonder what will happen if I don't get it? Mom will be upset, for one thing. I may not go to college—how would we pay for it? No college, no job. Pressure. Pressure. Pressure.

God's Perspective:
"I know the plans I have for you . . . to give you hope and a future" (Jeremiah 29:11).

Facing Jealousy . . .

She didn't mean it. I know she didn't mean it. But she said it anyway. "So how much did you pay Miss Bishop for your A in English? Strange that everyone else got C's." She's jealous. Just because she doesn't get A's in English and I do. Maybe if she'd study sometime instead of flirting with the guys . . .

God's Perspective:
"Each one should test his own actions. Then he can take pride in himself, without comparing himself to somebody else" (Galatians 6:4).

Feeling Unimportant When Friends Forget . . .

Stood up again. He promised to give me a ride home from work and there he goes, out the door with Sheila. Why should I be surprised? Someone else is always more important to him. In fact, someone else is usually more important to most of my friends. I wonder what it would feel like to be someone's best friend. I'll probably never know. So-called "friends." Forget their promises. Oh well.

God's Perspective:
"I have loved you with an everlasting love . . ." (Jeremiah 31:3). *"The one who calls you is faithful, and he will do it"* (1 Thessalonians 5:24).

Trying to Sleep . . .

Can't get to sleep. I could cut this dark with a knife. The phone didn't ring for me once tonight. Mom and Dad seem hurried and preoccupied. Wish I could talk to someone. Nothing here but the night. Guess I could try counting sheep . . .

God's Perspective:
"He grants sleep to those he loves" (Psalm 127:2). *"When I awake, I am still with you"* (Psalm 139:18). *Jesus said, "I am the good shepherd. The good shepherd lays down his life for the sheep . . . I know my sheep and my sheep know me"* (John 10:11, 14).

Ruth Senter

How's Your Attitude?

Take this self-inventory to see how your approach to life compares with God's view. For each situation, mark the number on the continuum that best represents how you'd respond.

1. When I wake up on Monday morning, I . . .
immediately dread all the same old things I have to do.   1—2—3—4—5   feel excited about a new day with new opportunities.

2. When I choose what to wear to school, I . . .
compare my clothes to others' clothes and feel awful.   1—2—3—4—5   want to look my best, but realize God sees me on the inside.

3. When my parents talk to me, I . . .
tune them out and wish they'd stop.   1—2—3—4—5   listen to them and try to learn from their experience.

4. When I feel inferior to others, I . . .
get so down I call myself degrading names.   1—2—3—4—5   remind myself that God values and loves me.

5. When I worry about failing, I . . .
just know that no matter how hard I try, I'll fail.   1—2—3—4—5   do my best anyway and know that my life is in God's hands.

6. When I face jealousy, I . . .
become sarcastic and put down people who are jealous of me.   1—2—3—4—5   am careful not to judge others.

continued

7. When I feel unimportant and friends break their promises, I . . .

become depressed and convinced that no one cares.   1—2—3—4—5   remind myself that God loves me and will keep his promises.

8. When I try to sleep, I . . .

stay awake and worry about all my problems.   1—2—3—4—5   praise God for being present with me, both when I'm awake and asleep.

How did you do? Add your total score and write it here:

    Total score: _____

The closer your total score is to 40, the closer your thoughts resemble God's. The lower your total score, the more you can improve your outlook!

Improving Your Outlook

Go back to the self-inventory and choose one situation you'd like to feel better about. Write it below. Then find Bible references from the article for the situation. Write them too.

Read the verses again, and think about God's response to the situation. Ask yourself: Why do I have a hard time with these circumstances? How do my responses compare with God's? What are two things I can do to improve my attitude and actions in this situation?

Write your ideas below.

For Example

Situation: *Listening to parents*

Bible verse(s): *Proverbs 1:8*

Ideas for improvement:

1. *Stop reading the cereal box and look at them when they talk to me in the morning.*

2. *Ask their advice on something at least once a week, and listen to what they say.*

Situation:

Bible verse(s):

Ideas for improvement:

1.

2.

Tell a Christian friend what you've written. Ask your friend for encouragement as you try to improve.

On small pieces of paper, write out the Bible verses that apply to the situation you've chosen to work on. Tape them to the mirror in your room or place them on your dresser. Every time you see the verses, say a short prayer for God's help in improving your responses.

And remember to thank God, too, when you begin to feel better about facing your problems!

Chapter 7
Down & Out & Feeling Blue

Last week your parents' yelling woke you up. They got louder and louder. You heard your mom say she wants a divorce. Since then you've felt depressed. When your mom asks what's wrong, you don't know what to say. You feel like crying.

□ □ □

Your sister Kelly used to write to you every week from college. Now she rarely writes—or calls. You miss her, so you call her. But she's too busy to talk. You hang up the phone. You feel like she doesn't care about you anymore.

□ □ □

Three weeks ago your girlfriend told you she wanted to date other guys. Now nothing seems to make any difference. You go through the motions of studying, being with friends and going to church. You feel sad all the time.

□ □ □

For about the last two weeks you haven't wanted to get out of bed in the morning. You don't want to eat. Nothing excites you anymore. School is okay, but you're not interested. You don't feel like hanging around your friends. You just want to be alone. Nothing terrible has happened. You just don't have any energy. Everything seems blah.

What's wrong? Most likely you're depressed. But don't worry. Everyone gets depressed at times. One university counseling center says as many as 40 percent of teenagers have a depression problem.

Signs of depression include feeling sad, lifeless and distant from people. Depression can range from feeling a little down to a deep sadness when you feel life isn't worth living. But no matter how depressed you are, you probably feel isolated. You feel separated from the people and things that make your life meaningful.

Some define hell as being separated from God. And that means being separated from the One who gives your life joy, meaning and excitement. Depression is similar. It's a feeling of isolation, sadness and frustration. It's like you can't get up the energy, excitement or courage to face life. And what's even tougher is the feeling of being far away from God.

▶ Recognize Depression

So what can you do about depression? There are no easy answers. What works for you may not work for others. So experiment. Try the suggestions in the "Depression Knockouts" box.

Depression Knockouts

How do you battle depression? Try these winners.

1. Write a letter to someone who would be surprised to hear from you.

2. Go to a park, a museum, a play, or somewhere you rarely think of going.

3. Watch a program on television that you wouldn't ordinarily watch—perhaps a new sitcom, or a PBS documentary.

4. Go see a movie.

5. Don't watch television for a whole day (better yet, don't watch for a whole week). Find out what radio has to offer, aside from your favorite music.

6. Bake bread or cookies from scratch.

7. Take a warm bath.

8. Take a hot shower.

9. Write all the things you really like to do. Don't stop until you've written a number at least equivalent to your age. If you're 17 years old you should be able to write 17 things you really enjoy. If you're 18, write 18 things. Then, without giving it much thought, do one of the things on your list.

10. Daydream without feeling guilty.

11. Fix or build something.

12. Write a poem.

13. Purchase a magazine you haven't read before and read at least two articles in it.

14. Create your own psychodrama. Act out a scene for at least 20 minutes that you would like to play in real life. Be very animated and enthusiastic.

15. Get a pet.

16. Munch a carrot very slowly.

17. Make a decision to collect something (stamps, coins, cactus plants).

18. Do something active. Play tennis, go to the park, or join an aerobics class.

From *When Living Hurts* by Sol Gordon. Reprinted with permission from Wesley Kolbe Publishing Company.

But before you can get rid of depression, you need to recognize the warning signs. People act differently when they feel down. When Bill feels down, he eats constantly. But Jean acts the opposite way; she stops eating altogether. Frank sleeps a lot when he's sad. But Cindy works, plays and never slows down when she feels blue.

How do you act when you feel down? When you recognize how you react to depression, you can begin to do something about it. Sometimes, though, it's tough to realize when you're feeling down because it sneaks up on you. And that's why it's important to have close friends.

► Talk With Friends

God has an incredible way of working through people. And friends are the best remedy for depression. When you feel blue, talk to your friends. Tell them how you feel. Ask them what they do when they feel down.

Karen makes good grades. She has plenty of friends and feels like life treats her well. But suddenly Karen starts snapping at all her friends. She stops eating. And she comes late to second-hour class.

Finally, Karen's best friend Jennifer asks Karen if her parents are still thinking about getting a divorce. Then Karen realizes what's going on. She's depressed about her parents. She tells Jennifer how she feels. And the more she talks, the better she feels. Things with her parents don't improve, but at least Karen doesn't feel alone anymore.

► Pray to God

When you begin feeling down, pray. Take some quiet time, and have a good, long talk with God. Tell him what's going on. Let God be your best friend.

Kevin usually is full of energy. Between school-work, band practice, church activities and friend-ships, he never has a minute to spare. But lately he looks tired and down. When anyone says anything, he brushes them off and mutters about needing a week of sleep.

Finally, he listens to his dad and slows down for a weekend. He rests. He takes a couple of long walks and does a lot of talking with God. Only after slowing down and praying does he remember that God loves him just as he is. Kevin realizes he doesn't need to be a superman to impress God.

Prayer is a powerful tool when it comes to depression. Kevin felt too busy to pray. But he needed prayer more than anything else. Praying helps you draw close to God. When you feel nobody understands, tell God. He always understands.

► Be Honest

Everyone feels depressed at times. It's part of being human. So when you tell someone your feelings, don't be embarrassed.

When you share your depression, say exactly how you feel. Are you sad, lonely, unhappy or bored? Or are you disappointed, frustrated or angry? When you name how you feel, you have a

No more Mr. Super Guy!

better chance of doing something about it.

But depression can be tricky. Most of the time depression leaves as fast as it comes. Sometimes it hangs around for a long time. Even if you've talked to a friend, rested, prayed and taken good care of yourself, you can still feel down. That's when it's time to talk to an adult.

Start with your minister. Talk to him or her. Share your feelings. If your minister can't help, chances are he or she will know someone who can.

Jim Smith-Farris

Section Two

Building Confidence: The Life You Live

Chapter 8

Attention: Who Wants It?

The business of trying to get attention is epidemic these days. Buckle your seat belt; let's scan the continent to catalog the latest attention-getters:

New Orleans: We're driving through a maze of one-way streets in the French Quarter when a guy oozes by with a pretty good dance step. Another skinny kid tap-dances on a sheet of plywood. They're getting noticed.

Santa Fe: It's sunset, and the central plaza in front of the Palace of Governors is barricaded from traffic. We watch the Santa Fe hard guys do wheelies in the empty streets around the square. One guy hangs his front bike wheel in the air down the whole side of the square, turns the corner, and keeps it up clear around the plaza. He's getting attention.

San Francisco: We're cruising Embarcadero near Fisherman's Wharf, and for blocks we watch eight kites hanging high in the bay breeze. When we get to the patch of grass at Pier 39, we see that a teenage girl has all eight kites attached to her one main string. We blow the horn and wave to her to let her know she got our attention.

Dallas: We stop for gas and I ask the guy who takes our gas money, "Who owns that fire-engine-red '48 Chevy pickup?"

"I do," he grins. "Great for picking up girls."

After our cross-country cruise, we pull up at your place. You hop out as I ask, "So what do *you* do for attention?"

Even if you usually feel that you *don't* want people to notice you, you probably daydream about situations in which you're the hero or the beauty everyone notices. Admit it: You like to be noticed.

► The Purpose of Attention

I'm sitting in Barfy's and you come in and tell me you need 15 bucks. "What for?" I say. "A pizza fix," you say. "Haven't eaten since yesterday and I'm starving for those little pepperonis." On the surface, you seem to need money. But what you *really* need is food in your stomach. You need something more than $15.

Attention-getting works the same way. Being noticed is what you seem to need on the surface. But what is it that you *really* need? Pull out one of your favorite daydreams: Imagine a room full of impressive people. Imagine the sounds, smells and colors. It's a night when you're looking perfect, and you've just done something spectacular—

which is the usual daydream situation, right? Now. Walk into the room. Every head turns; people seem surprised and you hear whispers of "Wow . . .!" Why does that attention feel so good? Right: because it carries a feeling of approval. When you get noticed, it's as if people are silently nodding, "Yeah, you're worth noticing."

But attention alone isn't much. Ever wish you could bask in the attention thrown at a rock star or model or athletic superstar? Ever hear how many of those celebrities grow to hate the attention? That's because people's attention doesn't always make the attention-getter feel genuine approval. The rock star knows most of the attention is due to the profession; the fans wouldn't want his autograph if he'd chosen the post office as a career. The model knows the attention will fade when her youth fades. The athlete knows the fickle public will forget him when his body quits performing up to expectations.

So realize that attention isn't what you really need. Knowing that you're approved of and important is the real *need*.

► Getting What You Need

You really don't need attention. So don't worry about getting the right jeans, about winning the Local Loudmouth Award, about being the teacher's Twinkie this year. You do need consistent, genuine approval, the kind that comes from God's consistent, genuine attention. Think it through:

● *God's attention is consistent.* "O Lord, you have searched me and you know me. You know when I sit and when I rise; you perceive my thoughts from afar" (Psalm 139:1-2).

He keeps such dedicated track of you that he knows exactly how many hair strands fell out during that last brushing. (See Matthew 10:30.) Since God is infinite, he can give you on-the-spot, 24-hours-a-day complete attention as if you're the only person in the universe.

● *God's attention gives genuine approval.* Most people think that when they do something wrong, God is shocked and suddenly despises them. It's as if they think God is surprised by anything. God knew a lot of your actions would be nasty before you were born, and yet he committed himself to loving you always (Jeremiah 31:3). Sometimes he doesn't approve of what you *do*, but he always approves of *who* you are.

God's approval of you isn't based on what you can do or what you look like. He approves of who you are because he made you.

When you check out how you look in the mirror and want to change your hair, your clothes or your face in order to get more attention, remind yourself: "I've got God's stamp of approval."

Don't be surprised at the effort it will take to work that phrase into your brain. Let yourself hear it over and over; write it on your mirror, inside your locker, on the bottom of your big toe. Doodle it in your notebook. After a while, you'll realize that getting people's attention isn't so important anymore. You won't have to try to *be* somebody; you'll realize you *are* somebody.

So that's it. Quit worrying about getting noticed. When you're watching everybody wear
themselves out grubbing for low-budget attention, relax. You don't need it. You know where
to get the genuine approval you *do* need. You
can be confident in who you are—whether or
not people notice. And if anybody *does* pay attention to you, enjoy it.

Bill Stearns

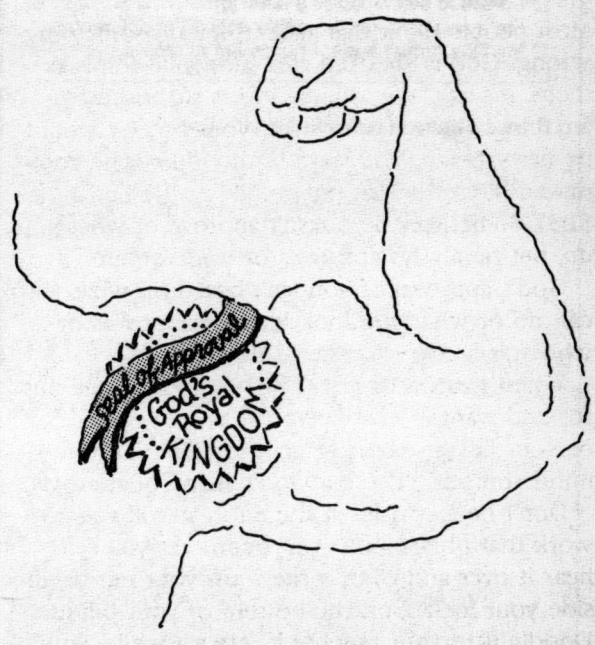

The only approval I require

What do you do to get attention? (Check the ones that apply.)

☐ I work hard on my hair. If I lost my hair, I'd die.
☐ I take risks with dare-devil stunts.
☐ I'm musical/athletic/artistic/intelligent; people notice my performances and accomplishments.
☐ I'm funny.
☐ I brag about what I've done, what I have, who I know.
☐ I bust heads.
☐ I dress to catch people's attention.
☐ I'm a non-conformist; people notice I'm different.
☐ My face turns heads; I guess I'm attractive.
☐ _____

Draw a picture of how you get attention.

Chapter 9
Pushover!

Arm Twisters

Before you dive into the chapter, read the arm-twisting situations below. For each, think how you'd respond; then write your response in the space provided.

1. It's 8 p.m. Tomorrow your physics teacher will give you the final exam. You haven't studied yet because you hate physics. But then your friend calls to invite you to Dairy Queen.
You:

2. It's Friday night. You're home alone for the weekend. Your parents won't come back until Sunday. They gave you explicit instructions to not let anyone visit. But your girlfriend calls. She wants to come over.
You:

3. You're scheduled to work until midnight tonight. You worked that late last night, and you're tired. Your friend calls, saying he has free tickets to a concert tonight. He tells you to call in sick.
You:

Now, read the chapter for some ideas on how to stand your ground without losing face.

Jess, who just came home from baseball practice, sits down at the dinner table with his family. The phone rings. It's Ron, Jess's best friend. "Jess, I know you just got home, but I need your help with today's math assignment right now," Ron says.

"I can't," Jess says. "I'm eating. And after dinner I need to work on my research paper that's due tomorrow."

"But, Jess, this is the only time I can do it," Ron pleads. "Please. I can't do it without you."

Jess finally gives in and drives to Ron's house without finishing his dinner. A week later, Jess angrily looks at his graded research paper. He knows it would have been two grades higher if he'd stayed home that night.

□ □ □

Cindy is changing clothes for tennis practice when several of her friends show up. "Cindy, we've decided to go to the mall and do a little guy watching," Lynn says. The others nod. "Please come with us."

"If I miss practice today, I can't play in the match tomorrow," Cindy says.

"We know you have practice," Lynn says. "But your coach won't bench you tomorrow just because you missed today."

Reluctantly, Cindy agrees to go with her friends. But as soon as they get to the mall, Cindy's friends meet some guys and take off. They leave Cindy behind.

The next day, the coach benches Cindy. She fights hard to hold back her tears. Then the coach announces that today's players will go on to regional competition. Again, Cindy's left behind.

► Postponing Plans

Do you ever feel like Cindy or Jess? You make a plan or set a goal. You work hard to accomplish it. Then someone asks you to do something else. And you do it, whether you really want to or not.

But when you postpone your plans, you hurt yourself. You end up with a lower grade on your research paper, like Jess. Or your coach benches you from the tournament, like Cindy. And when that happens, you kick yourself mentally. You want to do what you've planned, but someone makes you feel guilty for not doing something else.

It's obvious that Cindy and Jess should have said no. Their friends pulled them away from their original plans. But sometimes you can't pinpoint what keeps you from getting everything done that you wanted to.

Start by looking at the small time-eaters people ask you to do. "Come and run an errand with me." "Let's grab a Coke." "Let's go to a movie." These snatches of time add up to a lot of lost plans. So instead of getting mad at yourself for being such an easy pushover, take responsibility for your life. Learn how to say no and mean it.

► Saying No

Saying no seems simple. But it isn't. You'll always run into someone who will make you feel guilty if you say no. So how do you turn down people without losing their friendship?

● *Take time to evaluate.* Decide what's best for you now and in the future. Paul writes in 1 Corinthians 6:12: " 'Everything is permissible for me'—but not everything is beneficial."

So think about your decision dilemma. Will you be happy with your decision or disgusted with yourself? If Jess would have thought more about helping Ron, he could have decided not to help him. He could have figured out that not working on his research paper would have lowered his own grade. Look at the possible outcomes your choices can bring.

● *Keep saying no.* Say no to what you don't want to do. As new arguments, pressures and manipulations come up, evaluate each one. Then decide what's best for you.

If you continue to be asked to do something after you've already said no, simply repeat your answer. Don't give any excuse; you could end up arguing and feeling guilty about saying no. Just calmly keep saying no.

● *End the conversation.* If the pressure continues, get out of the situation. For example, Cindy could have said she was late to practice and she had to hurry. She could have stopped talking and headed to practice.

● *Remember that everybody has the right to personal time.* Even Jesus knew the importance of saying no. In Mark 6:30-32, Jesus and his disciples felt overwhelmed by the crowds. They didn't even have time to eat. So Jesus said no to the crowds. He and his disciples took time off for some much-needed rest.

How Not to Give In

How can you not give in? Try these techniques created by Sharon Scott, a licensed professional counselor:

- Change the subject.
- Ignore the request.
- Say you have to go.
- Tell a joke.
- Challenge the person to do it.
- Suggest another idea.

▶ Standing Firm

It's about three weeks into the summer. John finally feels he has his life organized so he can get everything done. After marching-band rehearsal and a college prep course, he has enough time to eat before going to work. Then after he gets home from work, he has enough time to keep up with his daily homework assignments. That leaves a few minutes for his daily phone call to his girlfriend, Lori. And he has Friday and Saturday nights open for dates and youth group events.

One day at lunch, Lori casually says to John: "Saturday morning we're stringing all the decorations for our family's barbecue that night. You'll be there, won't you?"

John thought about his research paper due Monday. "I need to spend Saturday morning at the library," he says. "I can't help with decorations."

"John, we need you," Lori pleads. "We don't have many dependable guys around. I'm counting on you."

"I'm sorry, Lori," John says. "I already planned to spend Saturday morning at the library. I can't help."

"John, sometimes you're so selfish," Lori says. "I think you don't care about me after all."

"I'm sorry it looks like I don't care," John says. "But I can't help you with the decorations. Now I need to get to band rehearsal. I'll call you tonight."

John could make up a number of excuses. Or he could get angry or try to make Lori feel guilty for asking him. But he doesn't. He sticks with his original decision. He doesn't swallow Lori's guilt trip when she says, "You don't care about me after all." Instead, John simply says that it appears that way. He says no again, and finally ends the conversation.

► Taking Charge

Learning to say no isn't easy. But you can learn how to say it without hurting others' feelings. Just keep practicing. So when someone wants to twist your arm, be like John. Say no. And feel good about taking charge of your life.

Mary Ann Visker

Chapter 10
Working Backward to Get Ahead

Take a dose of thinking ahead, a pinch of creativity and a dash of backwardness.

What do you get? The perfect formula for getting your act together.

It's simple. Working backward helps you get ahead.

In this chapter, we'll use the example of "Dirk," a guy who wants to plan ahead for college and improve his social life.

► 1. Set Your Final Goals First

Start by listing the major long-term goals you want to accomplish within the next eight months. Buy a spiral notebook and make your own personal planner like the "School-Year Personal Planner" example on page 77.

Dirk chose two long-term goals. He wanted to get a scholarship for college next year and he wanted to become less shy. So he wrote down his two long-term goals on a piece of paper.

Work on any goal. Think about your personality, your physical fitness, hobbies, activities, talents, homework, community projects and church commitments.

► 2. Determine Your Final Goal Date

Dirk found out scholarships are awarded in May. But his goal of not being so shy didn't have an obvious completion date. So Dirk chose April as the due date for his shyness goal. That way he could celebrate his accomplishments a month apart.

Finding out your final goal date is easy when you're aiming to try out for an athletic team, music group or other group. But it's tough when you plan to lose weight, learn how to speed read or get in shape.

Make sure you give yourself enough time to reach your goal. For example, if you want to lose weight, most doctors recommend losing no more than two pounds a week.

► 3. Set Weekly Goals

Before you can make weekly goals, you need to work backward. Break down your long-term goals into smaller ones. Before Dirk could apply for scholarships, he had to know what was available and get the applications.

To get over his shyness, Dirk also had to make

smaller goals. Dirk wasn't sure how to start. So he went to the library and found books on communication. Those books gave him some ideas on how to get over his shyness. Dirk then created a personal planner to start working backward.

Dirk started with his final goal date and worked backward to jot down weekly goals. By the time he completed this step, it was October 2, the week he wanted to begin working on his goal.

School-Year Personal Planner

Week	Dirk's Goals: Get scholarship and become less shy	Your Goals:
Sept.— week 1	Talk with parents about college. Meet and get acquainted with one new person at school.	
Sept.— week 2	Talk to pastor and youth minister about pros and cons of going to college. Go to youth fellowship meetings.	
Sept.— week 3	Meet with school counselor about college. After worship, say hello to someone I don't know at church.	

continued

continued . . .

Sept.— week 4	Write down life goals—and how college would help achieve them. Attend youth group retreat.
Oct.— week 1	Make tentative list of colleges to attend. Read book on communication tips.
Oct.— week 2	Write each college for admissions and scholarship information. Say hi to three new people.
Oct.— week 3	Write to English department chairperson for each college I'm applying to. Talk to someone of the opposite sex.
Oct.— week 4	Check with English teacher for possible English-major scholarships. Call three friends on the telephone.
Nov.— week 1	Plan to take ACT and SAT tests. Start a five-minute conversation with someone new each day.

continued

continued . . .

Nov.— week 2	Check with counseling center to find out possible local scholarships. Go on a group date.
Nov.— week 3	Ask for letters of recommendation from teachers and employers. Ask someone new to do homework with me.
Nov.— week 4	Enjoy Thanksgiving.
Dec.— week 1	Pick up letters of recommendation from teachers and employers. Decide who to ask to the winter dance.
Dec.— week 2	Apply for local scholarships. Join a pen-pal club. Begin writing letters.
Dec.— week 3	Apply for all specialty scholarships. Invite someone over to watch television.
Dec.— week 4	Apply for college scholarships. Give one of my new friends a Christmas gift. Enjoy Christmas.

continued

continued . . .

Jan.— week 1	Apply for English department college scholarships. Talk to seven people either on the telephone or in person.
Jan. 8- May 6	Wait for scholarship decisions. Invite a new friend to the amusement park with me. Celebrate!
May— weeks 2-4	Pick which scholarship to accept. Relax!

► 4. Set Daily Goals

For the week of October 9-15, Dirk noticed his personal planner said to write each college for admission and scholarship information. Dirk decided to apply to five colleges. He found the addresses and information about the colleges in *The Right College* by Arco Publishing, Prentice Hall Press, 200 Old Tappan Rd., Old Tappan, NJ 07675. You can also order it from your local bookstore.

Dirk chose to write to one college a day. He wrote the name of a specific college on a different day of his weekly calendar.

To work on his shyness, Dirk decided to say hi

Setting Goals

Here are a few tips on how to set workable goals. Refer to them as you plan out your calendar of goals.

Each goal should be:

● **Specific.** Make sure it's detailed enough. For example, don't simply say, "I will improve in German class"; say, "I will study German 45 minutes each school night."

● **Concrete.** Make sure it's down-to-earth. For example, don't say, "I will love my parents more"; say, "I will show more love to my parents by cleaning my room without being asked this week, and volunteering to wash the dishes two nights this week."

● **Achievable.** Make sure it's realistic. Don't say, "I will never miss another youth group meeting as long as I'm a teenager"; say, "I will attend my youth group meeting each week this month."

● **Measurable.** Make sure you have a specific time frame in which you'll want to have accomplished your goal. "I will write six letters to my friend in Kansas" is not as measurable as "I will write one letter each month to my friend in Kansas."

● **Personal.** Make sure you're in control of the success or failure of the goal. For example, don't say, "I will get a part-time job before summer"; say, "I will apply for a part-time job at McDonald's, Pizza Hut and Arby's before summer."

to one person on Sunday, Monday and Wednesday.

► 5. Celebrate!

When you reach your goals, treat yourself to something special. Give yourself a pat on the back for making your "backward" organization system work.

Dirk took one of the new friends he made during the year to a local amusement park. Not only did he have a blast riding the roller coaster, he enjoyed being with his new friend.

When Dirk got a scholarship in May, he celebrated by taking a weekend camping trip with one of his friends.

How about you? How will you celebrate when you make this backward organization plan work for you? Start thinking now. And then jump to it. You can get organized!

Mary Ann Visker

Determining Priorities

If you're feeling overwhelmed by the number of activities and tasks on your schedule, stop and prioritize. Analyze each item and decide whether it's really important.

List your activities and tasks according to:

● **Top priority.** These tasks are necessary to meet your goals. For example, if you've made a personal commitment to improve your spiritual life and you set a goal to have a 30-minute daily quiet time, then "daily quiet time" is a top-priority item for you.

● **So-so priority.** These tasks would be nice to accomplish, but you could do them later. For example, if you said you'd bake brownies for the youth group meeting on Sunday, but today's only Thursday, you could wait until tomorrow or Saturday.

● **Not-so priority.** These tasks do not contribute to your goals, and while you may want to do them, they do not *need* to be done now, tomorrow—or maybe ever. For example, if you'd like to rearrange your stamp collection, but you never take the time to do it, that's not a big problem.

Use this worksheet to help you rank the importance of your tasks and activities.

My Priorities List all the things you need or want to do: Check one:	TOP PRIORITY	SO-SO PRIORITY	NOT-SO PRIORITY

Chapter 11

The Procrastination Monster

Debbie had two weeks to finish an English essay, but she kept putting it off. The night before it was due, she finally started.

□ □ □

For weeks John put off the morning exercise he needed to get in shape for football. Two weeks before summer tryouts, John still hadn't started a daily exercise routine.

□ □ □

Don't ask Rochelle what caused the earthquake condition of her room. It just got that way. Although Rochelle vowed to clean up her room, she never got around to it.

□ □ □

Debbie, John and Rochelle have something in common. Something you may be familiar with. It's called procrastination—the art of putting off an unpleasant task.

Procrastination sneaks into your life without

warning. It can cause you to lose friends, your job and many opportunities. Procrastination can cause you to get a lower grade-point average. And that makes it hard to get into college.

The postponed studying and delayed writing assignments can make you worry. Some people even sink into depression. In short, procrastination can take the joy out of everything.

► The Ordeal Method

You can do something about procrastination. The method is called "the ordeal." By putting it to work, you can overcome procrastination with minimal effort.

The ordeal is a method used by family therapist Jay Haley. Its main requirement is that it must cause you at least as much stress as what you procrastinate. Find an ordeal (a detested chore) and attach it to something you put off. You'll soon stop procrastinating. But the ordeal must be good for you. It shouldn't hurt you in any way.

Debbie, John and Rochelle tried this method, and it worked! Debbie agreed that she'd either finish her English essay on time or wash her boyfriend's car. Debbie hates washing cars, so she completed her assignment in record-setting time.

John made a deal with his parents to clean the garage every night during his favorite TV show if he didn't exercise. The next morning John ran, lifted weights and did calisthenics for more than an hour.

Rochelle vowed to straighten up her room or

give up phone calls each night after supper.
When the phone rang, Rochelle ran to get it. Her
mother intercepted the call and took a message.
Rochelle hurried to her room to pick up papers
and hang up her clothes. Within a week, the
earthquake rubble disappeared.

► Procrastination Pointers

Debbie, John and Rochelle overcame their
procrastination by following a few tips. You can
too:

● *Make a list of ordeals.* Think of chores
you hate or activities you love to do and don't
like to give up. Your list may include cleaning,
weeding, mopping, mowing, not using the telephone, giving up television or not going to movies.

● *Apply an ordeal to your procrastination.*
Team up your chore with something you keep
putting off. You may choose to clean toilets if
you don't finish your homework on time.

● *Draw up a contract.* Make an agreement
with someone who can hold you to your word.
The written contract should state that if the task
isn't done by a certain time, you'll experience an
ordeal.

● *Reward yourself.* If you start the task on
time and fulfill your contract, reward yourself.
When Debbie finished her English essay, she
bought herself a new dress. John got an extra
mug of hot chocolate after each day's workout.
Rochelle bought a new telephone.

Other rewards include makeup kits, clothes, a
new hair style, eating out or spending a day in

the woods. Your reward should be affordable and make you feel good. The reward is a reminder that you're moving ahead. It's a way to pat yourself on the back.

● **Don't panic.** If you fail to do your task and must do your ordeal, don't panic. Think of the ordeal as a secret friend giving you motivational muscle. You may have to do the ordeal several times to convince yourself that you mean business.

● **Keep on trying.** If you don't do the task and find it impossible to keep your commitment to an ordeal, find a better one. Nancy, for example, kept putting off applying to colleges. Her ordeal of mopping the kitchen floor didn't work. She finally decided to mail her ex-boyfriend $25. "The idea of giving him my hard-earned money made me sick," she said.

The ordeal worked. Nancy completed every application. And she rewarded herself by going for a swim.

Although the ordeal can be a fun way to put off procrastination, the extra work doesn't create instant success. Ordeals demand commitment. If you keep trying and still can't stop putting off things—relax, be patient and accept yourself. Remember, admitting that you procrastinate is the first—and by far the most significant—step toward getting what you want out of life.

Sydney Harriet

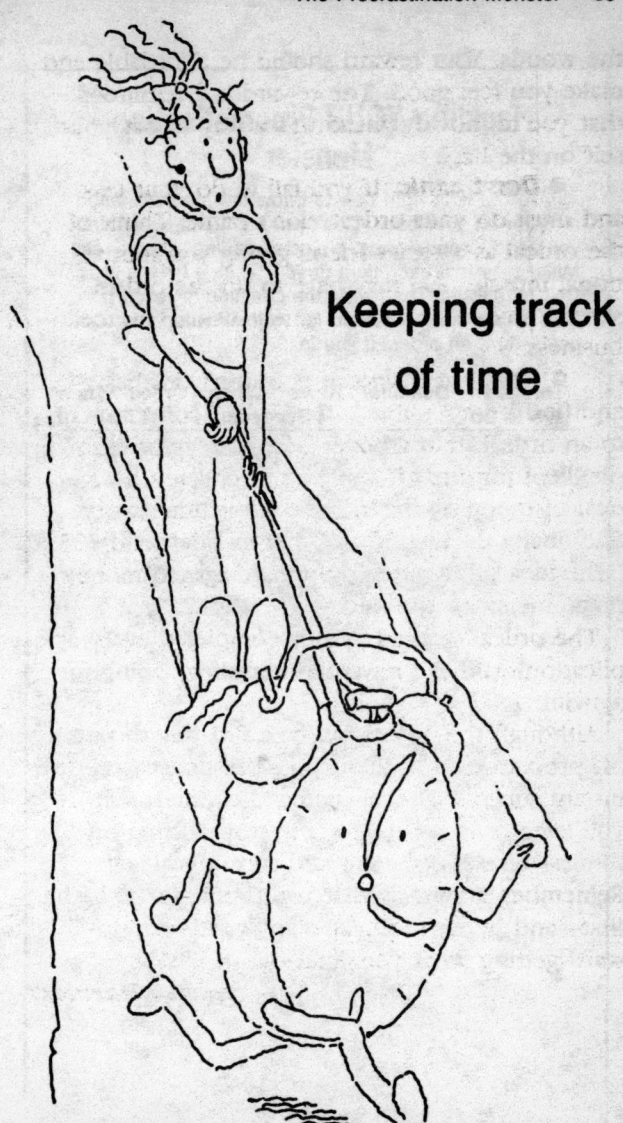

Keeping track
of time

Tackling YOUR Procrastination Monster

Take the time right now to throw the procrastination monster off your back. Don't put it off! List everything you need to do: reports, projects, reading, chores, etc. Make sure that each item under "Things I Have to Do" is realistic. Then write the deadline for each task. Remember to list a reward for yourself when you succeed—and an ordeal if you fail.

Things I Have to Do	Deadline	Reward When I Succeed	Ordeal When I Fail
1.			
2.			
3.			
4.			

Chapter 12
Overcoming Your Fear of Failure

"If only I could make the basketball team." "I wish I was good enough to ask a popular girl (or guy) out on a date." "I dream of being student body president." "I'd give anything to get the lead in the school play."

Do any of these sound like your favorite dream? We all have a special goal we'd love to reach. But most of our dreams end with doubt. We don't know if we can do it.

Most people avoid doing the one thing that can make their dreams come true. They don't give themselves the chance to fail.

► Take One Step at a Time
Picture a 10-month-old baby learning to walk. At first he or she takes one step, wobbles and falls. After crashing a few times, he or she can take three or four steps before stumbling.

What if that baby decides: "I'm not going to try walking anymore. Someone might laugh at me. I'm making a total fool of myself." What if that same baby five years later says, "I'm not going to run until I'm good at it."

Sound ridiculous? But is that different from the sophomore who says: "I'd love to get the lead in the school musical, but everyone will laugh at me if I try out for the part. Anyway, I know I could never make it in drama. So why should I try?"

Doing something well is a step-by-step process. Each step looks like a failure if you compare it to the final product. But each step is necessary to reach your goal.

You may try out for many parts in the school drama department. And you may get rejected many times before you finally land a small part. You take lots of drama classes. You look for places to act. And you gradually get over the fear of performing in front of people. Step by step, you learn it's fun to have people laugh at you and with you. You can never start at the bottom and suddenly end up on top. You need to struggle. You need to work your way up gradually.

If you want something, give yourself the chance to fail. Not once—but many times. Successful athletes will tell you that they lose more contests than they win. Babe Ruth was at bat 8,399 times. He hit 714 home runs, but he also struck out 1,330 times.

► Don't Give Up

Jesus could have looked at his life as a failure. He wanted people to learn how to live a life of love, compassion and understanding. But people turned him away. They laughed at him. They yelled at him. And they mocked him from the day he started teaching.

Jesus was jailed, beaten and crucified for trying to teach simple truths. But he never said, "I'm a failure." And because he didn't give up, his three years of teaching impacted the entire human race more than the teachings of any other individual.

Trying something new isn't easy. Moses felt he couldn't do the job God wanted him to do (Exodus 3:11; 4:10-13). Isaiah felt guilty and not good enough to do God's work (Isaiah 6:5-7). And like Moses and Isaiah, you may feel scared. But most of the fear seems to be of failing.

Even when you're afraid, keep trying. The only fool is the person who fails to try. Let Jesus be your example; get rid of the idea that only fools fail. And you'll find the key to success.

Mary Ann Visker

From Failure to Success

Americans believe Abraham Lincoln was one of the most successful presidents of the United States. But a closer look at Lincoln's life reveals years of failures, depression and pain. Look at his record:

1831—failed in business

1832—defeated for Illinois Legislature

1833—failed again in business

1835—sweetheart died

1836—suffered a nervous breakdown

1838—defeated for speaker

1840—defeated for elector

1843—defeated for House of Representatives

1848—defeated for House of Representatives

1855—defeated for Senate

1856—defeated for vice president

1858—defeated for Senate

1860—elected president

Lincoln's life demonstrates that failures need not hold us back. Ironically, we need failures to help us succeed in life. And, God helps us learn through failure. Take a moment to think of how God has helped you learn from failures in your life:

continued

1. Write some of your disappointments or failures in the cross below:

2. How has God helped you learn from those failures? Write your thoughts on the empty tomb:

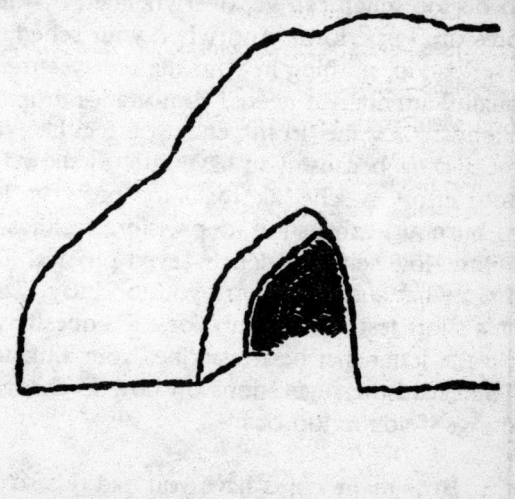

Chapter 13

Digging Yourself Out

Church. School. Sports. Family. Friends. Recreation. Clubs. Work. They all make demands on your time.

And sometimes meeting those demands becomes difficult—too difficult. Teenagers who try to do too much can get overwhelmed by the pressure to perform. And when your schedule is overloaded, nothing in your life receives the quality attention it needs. Your grades drop. Your friendships wane. In the end, you feel like you've messed up because you have little to show for all your effort. A schedule that's too busy can lead to burnout, exhaustion, depression, feelings of failure, low self-confidence—even physical illness.

So what about you? Are you too busy? Take this short test to find out. For each question, circle the letter that best describes your situation. Then read the suggestions on how to change things if you're too busy.

1. How many colds have you had this school year?

A. None or 1
B. 2 or 3
C. 4 or more

2. How many books did you read for fun in your spare time last year?
   A. 3 or more
   B. 1 or 2
   C. None

3. How many hours of sleep do you average each night?
   A. 8 or more
   B. 7
   C. 6 or fewer

4. How many meals did you eat with your family last week?
   A. 5 or more
   B. 3 or 4
   C. 2 or fewer

5. How many times in the last month have you fallen asleep someplace other than in your own bed?
   A. None
   B. 1 or 2
   C. 3 or more

6. How many times in the last month have you had to hurry in the morning because you slept too late?
   A. None
   B. 1 to 5
   C. 6 or more

7. How many times have you looked at your watch today?
   A. 0 to 5
   B. 6 to 10
   C. 11 or more

8. How many times this year have you canceled out on something you promised to do—because you ran out of time?
   A. None
   B. 1 to 3
   C. 4 or more

9. How many times in the last month have you been surprised by a test or assignment grade that was lower than you expected to get?
   A. None
   B. 1 to 3
   C. 4 or more

10. How many arguments have you had with your parents this week?
    A. None
    B. 1 to 3
    C. 4 or more

Now figure out your score. Give yourself 1 point for each A you circled, 3 points for each B and 5 points for each C. Then add up your total points. Use the scale below to evaluate your score.

► 10-17 Points

Yea! Your schedule isn't too busy. In fact, it seems like your activities aren't a problem for you. But take time to evaluate your schedule. Is it balanced? Do you spend a lot of time in front of the tube?

Remember that boredom can lower your confidence level just as effectively as over-activity. Either way you feel like you're not accomplishing anything. Look for extracurricular activities you enjoy. Volunteer at your church or school.

If you feel good about your balanced schedule, give yourself a pat on the back. Congratulations!

► 18-26 Points

Not bad. You probably find that life clips along at a steady, yet challenging pace. Sometimes it gets extremely busy, sometimes it doesn't.

Take advantage of those not-so-busy times by relaxing, reading or talking with your friends and family. Think carefully before you add other commitments to your schedule.

► 27-34 Points

You're busy. Sometimes, very busy. Your schedule stays full most of the time, and you're rarely bored.

Usually you handle your many commitments well. But sometimes you feel overwhelmed.

Don't add anything to your schedule unless you drop an activity you're already doing. Plan now for some free time in the near future. Sleep in on Saturday. Plant some flowers. Go window-shopping at the mall. Spend an evening at home with your family. Do something you've been meaning to do for a long time. The sense of freedom or accomplishment you'll feel will be great!

Make sure you're in control of your schedule rather than letting it control you.

► 35-50 Points

Whoa! Chances are that you're buried under commitments. You're probably tired and feeling lousy about yourself. If so, try the following plan:

1. Take a day off immediately. Cancel all your extracurricular activities. Make apologies where necessary.

2. Spend time taking stock of what things in your schedule represent important personal goals. What's motivating you to attempt to do so much? What do you hope to accomplish? Fill in your list of activities according to these categories:

- Things I do because they're fun.

- Things I do because I have to.

- Things I do because others say I should.

● Things I do because they'll benefit me in the future.

● Things I do because they'll benefit others.

3. Look at the lists with a critical eye. Are they lopsided in any way? Is any category much longer than the others? What can you change to create balance in your schedule?

4. Realize that you can't do everything. Trying to do too much only makes you feel frustrated or incompetent. Drop some activities from your schedule. It's easier to quit something you've just begun than something you've almost completed. It's also easier to drop something that will affect only a few people rather than something that affects many.

When you decide what to drop, drop it completely. Don't be wishy-washy. Don't say you'll help out. Don't say you'll keep doing it until your replacement is found. Make a clean break. And spend your time completing other projects, not worrying about the things you decided not to do.

5. Be careful about new commitments. Things that look fun from a distance can create added pressure when they're crammed into an already

overstuffed calendar. Make room in your schedule for rest, recreation, family, friends and God.

Plan according to what's most important to you, not what you think others expect from you. You'll end up feeling better about the things you do—and about you!

Dean Feldmeyer

When Christ Got Tired

You're not the only one to face a packed schedule. As word spread about Jesus' healing power, crowds started following him around.

What did Christ do when the crowds threatened to overwhelm him? Read the following scripture passages. Think about how you can follow Christ's example when your life gets too hectic.

● Mark 6:45-46—"Immediately Jesus made his disciples get into the boat and go on ahead of him to Bethsaida, while he dismissed the crowd. After leaving them, he went up on a mountainside to pray."

● Luke 5:15-16—"Yet the news about him spread all the more, so that crowds of people came to hear him and to be healed of their sicknesses. But Jesus often withdrew to lonely places and prayed."

● John 4:4-6—"Now he had to go through Samaria. So he came to a town in Samaria called Sychar, near the plot of ground Jacob had given to his son Joseph. Jacob's well was there, and Jesus, tired as he was from the journey, sat down by the well. It was about the sixth hour."

Chapter 14

Making Life Decisions

Imagine you are forced to give away three future personal decisions. This means you won't be able to choose for yourself; someone else will tell you whom you'll marry, where you'll go or what you'll do.

Which three choices would you give away?

- your life career?
- whom you'll marry?
- how many children you'll have?
- what college you'll attend?
- what books to read?
- whether you must serve in the military?
- what church you'll attend?
- what car to buy?
- where you'll live?

How would you react if you really had to give away those choices? You might say: "Forget it! I'm not giving away any of my decisions—even if someone else would tell me what to do!"

You might feel relieved.

Or maybe you secretly wish you *did* know a trustworthy expert who could make all your decisions for you.

Any of those responses might be honest if you believe you don't know how to make your own decisions.

Learning decision-making skills brings countless benefits. Would you like to be less vulnerable to pressure? Do you want to feel more comfortable with yourself? Would you like to know where you're going in life? If you answered yes, then practice these skills and learn to become your own decision-maker.

► Choose the Decisions You'll Make Yourself

Making good decisions takes time. And it requires a lot of thought and study. There simply isn't enough time to make all decisions carefully. So, the first decision-making skill is choosing which of your personal decisions you want to keep for yourself. Then give the rest away. Sound awful? It isn't. This is actually the way to take charge of your life.

Some personal choices you might decide to keep include your career, friends, Christian faith and use of leisure time. Some choices you might throw away could include what route you'll take to school, the week's dinner menu or how much time you'll talk on the phone. Which choices do you want to control? Which decisions do you want to let go of? Start the process of decision-making by choosing the decisions you want to make yourself.

► Decide Who You Want to Become

Consider the amount of time you spend thinking about what's wrong with you as a person. Wouldn't this time be better utilized thinking about the kind of person, friend or Christian you want to be? Don't give those personal-quality decisions away. And don't overlook the importance of these in learning decision-making skills.

List 10 personal qualities you would like to develop:

Personal Qualities I Want

1.

2.

3.

4.

5.

6.

7.

8.

9.

10.

Those who decide the kind of person they want to become can respond to the daily need to make emotional and moral decisions. When faced with a pressured decision, those people ask: "How will I feel about myself tomorrow? Will I be able to respect myself if I do this? What price will I pay with my choice?"

Decide the kind of person you want to be by observing others. Look closely at the friends you respect. Talk to parents and adults whose values and choices you admire. Study God's Word. Pray and spend time in meditation and reflection. You'll never be your own decision-maker unless you decide who you want to be.

► Explore What You Value

Making decisions is really choosing among values. Those who know what they value don't have to struggle with their decisions. Their values become their guide in selecting the best options. But most high school students don't know what they really value, so decisions are tough.

Because most values are more accurately reflected by what we *do* rather than by what we *say*, use this exercise to determine what you really value.

Since you won't be showing this to anyone, be honest with yourself. Take a notebook with you for one week. Jot down exactly how you spend every hour. Include everything—standing around, brushing your teeth, looking in the mirror. At the end of the week, total the minutes and hours spent on different things. Then compare this

---

Values List

Make a list of what you value:
(Example: time with friends, exercise, good grades, music, etc.)

_____

_____

_____

_____

---

with your prepared list of values. What's the result? How does your time differ from your list? Were you surprised or shocked by what was revealed in the time sheet? Do you want to make changes in the week ahead? How will you use your time differently? What does this list reveal about your values?

► Examine All Possible Consequences

What do you do when you're faced with a decision in which the alternatives seem equally appealing? Here's an exercise that can help you decide when both solutions seem to be okay.

Write each option on a separate sheet of paper. For each option, list on one side positive and on the other side of the paper negative possibilities for the action. Don't hesitate to turn to others you respect in preparing the lists.

When finished, study each option, looking first at the negative, then at the positive possibilities. Next, compare your most important rankings on each paper. As you finish this process, you'll realize which choice is best for you.

► Decide Where You Want to Go

Many people approach major life-decisions by considering the options before they've decided their destination. Perhaps that's the most common and most serious mistake of some decision-makers. To make your own decisions, first decide your goals or desired outcomes.

Then examine your alternatives or find new ones. Knowing where you're going gives you a basis for evaluating available paths.

When you leave high school, you'll be at a crossroad. You've probably already asked others what path you should take. Perhaps you've struggled with college versus job; one career option versus another; marriage versus college or a job. But as you've considered all these routes, have you thought where you want to be in five or 10 years? When you deliberately plan ahead, you can eliminate certain paths.

Deciding your destination isn't easy. Many unknowns lie ahead; there's so much you don't know about yourself. But goal-setting is a life-determining task that's worth the struggle. Discipline yourself by setting weekly and monthly goals.

Use this experiment. Decide how to spend the

Which way to happiness?

My Goals

Next week:

Next month:

Next year:

The next five years:

The next 10 years:

---

next week, month or beyond. After each period of time, evaluate. Did you follow your goals?

Decision-making is hard work. It requires thought about who you are as a person and the quality of life you want to live. If you decide to be your own decision-maker, you'll find yourself overcoming indecision and uncertainty. You'll be moving in a direction that leads to adult life with greater confidence, self-respect, enjoyment and satisfaction.

Take the time.

Make the effort.

You'll enjoy the rewards of good decisions!

Barbara Varenborst